Genre  Historical Fiction

**Essential Question**
How do shared experiences help people adapt to change?

# THE PICTURE PALACE
BY RACHEL HAYWARD
ILLUSTRATED BY DAVID OURO

**Chapter 1**
The Call of the Movies ............... 2

**Chapter 2**
Shirley Temple ....................... 5

**Chapter 3**
Washing Windows.................... 8

**Chapter 4**
Bank Night ...........................11

**Respond to Reading** ................ 16

**PAIRED READ** The Golden Age of Hollywood.. 17

**Focus on Genre** .....................20

## CHAPTER 1
# THE CALL OF THE MOVIES

Frank and Joey were arguing about movie heroes. It was the same argument they always had, but they never got tired of it.

"Tarzan could not beat King Kong," scoffed Joey. "King Kong is stronger."

"But Tarzan is smarter," said Frank. "He would know how to tame King Kong."

Walking around the corner, they saw a billboard for *Call of the Wild*, a movie starring Clark Gable.

"We have to see that movie," said Joey. But they would **obviously** need to buy movie tickets. "We need moolah to buy tickets," said Frank gloomily. Those days, money was hard to get.

Frank could remember the time before the stock market crash in 1929, six years ago. He and his parents lived in a big house with a yard. Dad ran a factory and often came home with candy in his pocket or flowers for Ma.

Then the crash came, and Dad's factory went out of business. They had to sell the house, and Dad got a low-paid job in a department store. Frank knew they were luckier than some. Joey's family couldn't pay their rent sometimes, and at least twice this year, their belongings had been thrown out on the sidewalk.

Joey said, "We need a money-making plan."

Frank spotted a woman selling apples on the sidewalk. "We could sell things," he suggested.

"What could we sell?" asked Joey. He pointed out a man washing a shop window. "What about washing windows?"

Frank grinned. "Mrs. Fisher next door might lend us some buckets. She said you're as cute as a bug's ear." Frank **sprinted** down the street, laughing as he ran.

**STOP AND CHECK**

Why are Joey and Frank trying to earn money?

## CHAPTER 2
# SHIRLEY TEMPLE

Frank's little sister, Marie, was waiting for him when he arrived home with Joey.

She asked, "Want to play jacks, Frankie?"

Frank loved playing with Marie, but he didn't want Joey to think he was a **weakling**.

"I'm busy," he said. "We're looking for jobs." Marie's lip wobbled. To Frank's surprise, Joey sat down with Marie and started playing.

"I'll play," he said, "but I'm a beginner. You'll have to go easy on me!"

Joey and Marie were soon absorbed in their game. Disappointed that Joey was focused on Marie, Frank **slouched** into the kitchen.

A few moments later, Marie skipped in with Joey behind her. "Joey and Frankie are getting jobs!" she announced.

Ma frowned at Frank.

"Just part-time," he explained **hastily**, before Ma could say no. She disapproved of kids quitting school early. "We need money to see *Call of the Wild*."

"With Clark Gable," added Joey.

Ma's expression changed. "Clark Gable?" she said dreamily. "Well, I guess that's okay then."

"Is Shirley Temple in it?" Marie asked. The curly-haired movie star was Marie's **heroine**. She loved her! Every Saturday night, Marie insisted on having her hair wound up in rags so she could be "curly like Shirley."

"Have a sandwich, Joey," said Ma. She looked with worry at Joey, who was wearing a frayed, hand-me-down shirt and shoes with holes. "Take two!" she said.

That evening, when Dad came in to say good night, Frank asked, "Is it wrong to want money for the movies when people have lost their jobs and homes?"

Dad shook his head in **sympathy**. "Don't worry," he said. "Movies remind us that dreams are still possible. As long as we have enough to live, it's safe to **assume** that I approve of you earning money for the movies."

**STOP AND CHECK**

Why is Frank worried about spending money to go to a movie?

7

## CHAPTER 3
# WASHING WINDOWS

Getting work was hard. Frank and Joey knocked on doors for an hour without success. No one wanted to pay to have their windows washed.

"The people here don't have money," said Joey. "Let's go across town to the big houses."

It was a long, tiring walk, but Frank didn't complain. He wanted to prove he was a guy Joey could **rely** on.

Finally, they stopped outside a big brownstone. When Joey rang the bell, a woman answered.

"Morning, ma'am!" said Joey. "We were admiring your windows, and we said, 'If we washed them, they could look even better.'"

Frank nodded, trying to look **supportive** of his friend.

"A fellow cleaned my windows last week," the woman replied. "Try across the street!"

The boys were knocking on the door across the street when a **gruff** voice shouted angrily, "This is my block! Take a hike!"

Frank was scared, but Joey yelled back, "You don't own the street!"

The man was holding a bucket. "I have mouths to feed." Frank and Joey ran away.

Back in their own neighborhood, they stared at the movie billboard again.

"We'll never see that movie," Joey said gloomily.

They were interrupted by a cry. A man with a briefcase had crashed into a boy on a bike. As the briefcase went flying, papers blew across the street. Quick as a flash, Joey ran after them and returned them to the man.

"You're fast on your feet!" the man said. "You'd be hard to beat at Bank Night."

"What's Bank Night?" Frank asked.

"It's a competition at the Palace Theater," the man explained. "You write your name, and if they pull it out of the box, you have 60 seconds to get up on stage and claim a five-dollar prize. But there's no **guarantee** that your name will be chosen."

"A five spot!" Joey sighed. "What do you say, Frank?"

"What have we got to lose?"

"Bank Night, here we come!" said Joey.

> **STOP AND CHECK**
>
> What does the man with the briefcase tell Joey?

## CHAPTER 4
# BANK NIGHT

The boys arrived at the Palace Theater early on Bank Night, but there was already a long line. Although Frank had been to the Palace before, the **elaborate**, fancy decorations still took his breath away. The colorful, painted ceiling and the gold statues were beautiful!

At the ticket booth, a young man wrote their names on slips of paper and slid the paper through a slot in a box. Then the boys joined the **throng** of people crowding into the theater.

Inside, the theater was already full. The boys waited nervously.

The lights dimmed, organ music began to play, and a spotlight lit the stage. The theater manager stepped out carrying the box, which he put down beside a large clock.

"Welcome to Bank Night!" he shouted. "If I call your name, you have 60 seconds to claim your prize! I'll try three names, and if no one wins, no prize!"

He unlocked the box and pulled out a slip of paper. The organ music grew louder.

"Bob McNeill!" shouted the manager. He hit a button, and the clock started ticking.

A man leaped up. People tried to scramble out of his way, but he was only halfway to the front when the clock reached 60 seconds.

The manager drew another name.

"Joey Mitchell!"

Joey gasped. "RUN!" Frank yelled, but Joey could not get through the crowd. "Go low!" Frank shouted.

Joey dropped and began to worm his way around people's legs. The clock ticked—45, 46, 47 seconds—then Joey reached the stage and threw himself at the manager's feet.

The crowd went wild, but the manager shook his head. "No kids!"

Frank felt sick. They had come so close! Then a voice called, "But his name was in the box!"

"Give the kid the prize!" another yelled.

"I don't make the rules," the manager said, but the crowd began to boo and chant, "The kid gets the prize!"

The manager **glared** angrily at the crowd for a moment, but then he pulled a five-dollar bill from his wallet and gave it to Joey. Everyone cheered.

Outside the theater, Joey looked dazed. "Thanks, Frank," he said. "I **nominate** you for best pal award."

"Hey, Speedy," a voice called. It was the man with the briefcase. "I'm in the newspaper business, and a boy as quick as you would make a great paper boy. What do you say? You will deliver papers one hour a day, six mornings a week, and the pay is a dollar a week."

Joey nodded. The man wrote down an address. "See you on Monday, Speedy. Don't be late!"

"Five dollars and a new job," Joey said. "This might be the best day of my life!"

> **STOP AND CHECK**
>
> How does the man with the briefcase help Joey?

## Summarize

Summarize *The Picture Palace*. Use the most important details from the story. Your graphic organizer may help you.

## Text Evidence

1. Reread Chapter 1. Compare and contrast Frank's family with Joey's family. Use examples from the text to help you answer.
   **COMPARE AND CONTRAST**

2. Look at the word *belongings* on page 4. What does it mean? Use clues from the paragraph to help you figure it out.
   **VOCABULARY**

3. Reread Chapter 3. Write about how Frank and Joey react to events. How are they the same? How are they different?
   **WRITE ABOUT READING**

**Genre** | **Expository Text**

**Compare Texts**

Read about how going to the movies helped people during the 1930s.

# THE GOLDEN AGE OF HOLLYWOOD

The Great Depression was a terrible financial crisis. It lasted from 1929 to 1939. Many people were very poor.

During this difficult time, the movies gave people a place to gather with others. People could escape from the harshness of their daily lives at the movies.

Before the Depression, most movies were in black and white. Movies had no sound. Instead, musicians played in theaters. By the late 1920s, movie studios made color "talkies." These movies had spoken dialogue and sound effects.

Some movies during the Depression showed how difficult life was for people. For example, gangster movies showed violence and poverty.

However, musicals and romances showed a different world. Screwball comedies also became popular. These were funny movies with unexpected plots and unlikely romances.

## The Great Depression

The Great Depression started in the United States on October 29, 1929. The stock market crashed on that day. Many people lost a lot of money when the price of stocks fell. Some businesses closed and thousands of people lost their jobs. In 1933, 25 percent of people couldn't find work.

During the Great Depression, soup kitchens were common. Soup kitchens served meals to people who could not afford to buy food.

Some of the movie theaters built in the 1920s and 1930s were very grand. They became known as "picture palaces." They had soft, plush seats, velvet curtains, and gold decorations.

To get people to come to the movies, many theaters had special offers. Some held Bank Nights, where people could win prizes.

A short newsreel and a cartoon usually played before the main movie. Sometimes there was live music. A night at the movies was an escape from daily life.

Radio City Music Hall was built in 1932. It was the largest theater in the United States at the time it opened.

### Make Connections

How did watching movies together help people in the 1930s? ESSENTIAL QUESTION

Joey and Frank are going to see a movie. Describe their experience. TEXT TO TEXT

# Focus on Genre

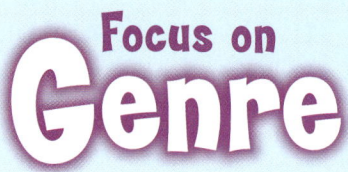

**Historical Fiction** Historical fiction tells a story about people or events from the past. It can have real or made-up characters and events. Historical fiction has a setting, characters, and a plot.

**Read and Find** On page 2 of *The Picture Palace*, the author tells us when the story is set. The illustrations show where the story is set, how people dressed, and other details of daily life.

## Your Turn

Work with a partner. Find an illustration in *The Picture Palace* that shows life in the 1930s. Now recreate the drawing. Your drawing should show the same scene, but today. What would be the same in the drawing? What would be different now? Use your imagination. Include lots of details. Share your drawing with your group.